MW01222602

CONFESSIONS OF A CAR SALESMAN

By

MICHAEL ACKERMAN

PublishAmerica
Baltimore

© 2008 by Michael Ackerman.
All rights reserved. No part of this book may be reproduced, stored in a retrieval system or transmitted in any form or by any means without the prior written permission of the publishers, except by a reviewer who may quote brief passages in a review to be printed in a newspaper, magazine or journal.

First printing

PublishAmerica has allowed this work to remain exactly as the author intended, verbatim, without editorial input.

ISBN: 1-60672-543-2
PUBLISHED BY PUBLISHAMERICA, LLLP
www.publishamerica.com
Baltimore

Printed in the United States of America

Dedication

This book is dedicated to
my loving wife and family.

They are the reason I get up every day and do what I do.

A Note from the Author (That's Me!)

Bless me Father for I have sold. It has been seven years since my last confession, but not my last commission. I committed the ultimate sales sin by being lured in by the Great Satan. Car sales. Is there any salvation for the unrepentant? What did you say Father? I couldn't possibly say that many *Our Fathers* and *Hail Mary's*! Maybe I'll just write a book.

Confessions of a Car Salesman is no Homer's *Odyssey* or vain search for redemption or validation. It's just a series of experiences in the subculture of automotive retailing. It started out as a therapeutic exercise for my own amusement and sanity and quickly grew into larger writing exercise. It is something akin to writing in a diary or telling your wife or friend about your day. Sometimes it's humorous. Sometimes it's enraging and sometimes it's just plain bizarre. But despite what preconceived notions you have about me as a car salesman, sales manager or car sales in general, I hope you'll find something to relate to because car salesmen put on their pants one leg at a time just like you.

If you have ever had a boss that made you crazy and stressed or a fellow employee that helped you get through the week, you'll find *Confessions of a Car Salesman* is more like real life than even I could have imagined. Henry Davis Thoreau may have wrote "we lead lives of quiet desperation" (that's right, a car salesman knows who Thoreau was), but we also lead a life of quiet selling too. Even if you disagree with that idea you would try to "sell" me on the merits of your point of view and that makes you a salesperson too. The world's "oldest profession" is actually a form of sales making sales the world's true oldest profession.

I've reached a point in my life where I have time to take stock of what I've become and it's not too hateful. My youngest are going off to college soon and it will just be my wife and I. And when things seem like things are all too much to handle, I remember that she's going to spend the rest of her life playing

Scrabble with an aging, out-of-shape car salesman. That instantly makes me feel better because DAMN does her outlook suck!

Why is this book an important piece of literature? Simple, it's not, and that's taken a lot of pressure off me. Until the contract I signed had a deadline. Now I spend hours just staring at the computer screen reading what I have written and second guessing myself. I've sold the idea of the book and now I have a deadline to be witty and clever (Scrabble with an old car salesman, Scrabble with an old car salesman, Scrabble with an old car salesman.) Okay, I feel better now. Enjoy!

Table of Contents

How Did I Get Here

I was sitting at the kitchen island in the house we built just a year before on a stool I had made myself. My head was in my hands with what felt like the weight of the world on my shoulders. I had just closed one of our art gallery/ stores after seven years of being self-employed and the last would soon follow. Everyone in the house was steering clear of me knowing how depressed I was. It was one of those times when the silence was so loud it hummed in my ears. Our home was a house of six people that was always bustling with kids yelling, playing and watching television, but tonight it remained eerily quiet. Just the newly installed halogen track lighting lit my ominous space. That's when my daughter, who was only four years old climbed up on the stool next to me. She knelt on the stool and rested her head on my shoulder. I did my best not to look too distraught, but I wasn't very successful. With both of us staring forward at the new double ovens that were just installed she asked "What's the matter Daddy?" Let see, how much could a four-year old mind comprehend? Maybe I should just say "Nothing honey" and hope that it will satisfy her curiosity and I can continue to sit and wallow in my self-pity. Deciding to tell a brief version of the truth, I told her Daddy was just a little sad about closing his stores. That's when she said what would become my mantra for the next several years. Without hesitation she said, "I know how you feel. Don't think about it."

At that point in time I didn't think there was anything that could be said that would make me smile, but she did it. I didn't think it was possible, but there I was. The financial bottom was falling out and I sat there with this stupid grin on my face. Don't think about it. Could it really be that easy? Others familiar with my situation gave me sage advice like "It's for the best", "Try not to worry yourself sick" and my personal favorite, "When God closes a door, He opens a window." Unless the window was high enough to jump out of, I wasn't interested. The part of her statement, "I know how you feel" was so innocent because she couldn't possibly understand what I was going through. Still, it made me smile, but "Don't think about it." That was pure gold. It's as if she gave me permission to think about what could be next.

The next day I was at my last open store alone with the classified section looking for work. My wife had already decided to go back to college. A CD that we sold in the store played in the back round. I had it heard so many times before and now I couldn't wait to sell the last one so I would never have to hear again. I had been in retail my whole life and I wasn't even sure what I was looking for. **WANTED: A failed business owner to be paid large sums of money while he works through his self-esteem issues.** Nope, nothing like that in here. Though one ad did catch my eye; **GAURANTEED $40,000 per year. Will train. No experience preferred.** It was an ad for a car dealership about 45 minutes from home. My oldest brother had sold cars since he got out of the service and always told me that it beats working for a living. $40,000 a year guaranteed. That would just cover the bills. It's far enough away that I wouldn't know anyone. God forbid that I would want anyone to know I was selling cars. After all, I watch television and I see how they are in the movies. $40,000 a year, guaranteed. Chrysler, Plymouth, Dodge, Jeep and Eagle. Am I dating myself? Plymouth and Eagle aren't even built any more. At the speed I'm writing this book, The Chrysler Corporation may not even be around by the time I get my fat book deal. $40,000 a year guaranteed. So without even telling my wife I went to fill out an application for what I know now was all the wrong reasons to get into the car business. $40,000 a year guaranteed!

My application and resume boasted about a successful businessman with eons of management experience. A real go-getter with a can-do attitude. Self-motivated with a drive to succeed. What a bunch of crap, but that sounded better than saying I was down on my luck and I was reluctantly willing to try my hand at car sales until something better came along. When I got called for an interview I decided to tell my wife what I was thinking about. She would have to cover the store until the lease was up in May and it was only February. I shouldn't have been surprised that she was supportive. We loved each other and the last couple years had taken a toll on both of us and the $40,000 guarantee resonated well. There were six mouths to feed after all and the bill collectors were calling. We were running out of time and excuses and maybe some of you know what I'm talking about.

I dusted off a suit I hadn't worn in seven years and got the job. I did it! I got the job. Maybe I was a desirable employee! When I showed up for the first day of training I saw that twelve other people who were just as desirable as I was. You know that sound effect they use they use on game shows when you get the answer wrong, "whah, whah, whaaaah." That's what I heard in my head as I entered the room. The training room was above a service garage and looked like it had been frozen in time since about 1972. Worn commercial carpet that was a hard-to-describe shade of blue and blonde colored fake wood, or should I say "faux" wood paneling that was warped, peeling and broken in spots. Three folding tables formed a "U" shape in the center of the conference room and they were lined with mismatched chairs and a make-shift podium from which we were to be lectured on the finer points of the automotive retail industry. And you know that $40,000 guarantee? By the end of my first day I realized that if I didn't make at least that much, the only guarantee I had was that I wouldn't have a job. But it was too late now so I had to screw my head back on straight and start learning about this sub-culture that few knew existed.

One of the first things I learned was that you didn't have to lie to sell cars. In fact, the best salespeople never lied, omitted or stretched the truth. So far, so good. I spent the remainder of the next two weeks learning about the product, participating in the dreaded role-playing and gravitating toward the more professional people in our group. A failed hearing aid salesman, a failed preacher and a failed teacher. How do you fail at preaching? They were pretty good guys, except the preacher. The more I got to know him, the more he creeped me out. Don't get me wrong. I'm a "cradle Catholic" with nothing against religion, but I don't know what kind of church would have this guy. Anyone who says God wants him to sell cars is couple fries short of a happy meal. Cure AIDS, feed the poor, shelter the homeless maybe. But sell cars?! Nah, I'm not buying it. It was an eclectic group of guys to be sure. As I write this, I am the only one of the four that is still in the car business.

I hit the floor on cold and rainy Saturday in March and staked claim to an office that I shared with the ex-teacher I trained with. It had one phone, a round table with three chairs and an old dented, two-drawer filing cabinet. It measured about six-by-six feet and if we weren't talking to each other, we were in each other's way. Not exactly the corner office suite, but it would have to do. I unceremoniously put my name in the rotation and at around 10:30 a.m and at 11 a.m. I had greeted my first customers. They were a young couple with no children looking for a good used economy car. I asked all the questions

I could remember to ask, listened to their answers and needs, and then it happened. I sold a used Plymouth Neon, I started to make some money and I started to have some fun. Fun and work aren't normally in the same sentence, but I started to feel a glimmer of hope. Enough hope to keep me here.

It's Cooler to Say "I'm Married to a Writer"

"It would be cooler to say I'm married to a writer than a car salesman". That's what my wife said when I started to work on this book! I've been in the car business for over ten years and that's what she says now?! Truthfully, I have felt the same way at times. I guess it was the elephant in the living room that no one wants to talk about. But why is that? I'm fair with my customers. I don't have to duck into another isle at the grocery store or avoid someone at church if they're a past customer. Although, a neighbor called me at 7:00 a.m. on a Sunday morning to tell me that he was in Canada and hit a moose with the SUV I sold him. He wanted to know what I was going to do since he had bought the vehicle from me. I told him to sober up, call the police and then call his insurance agent. I was going back to sleep.

The car business has sent us to tropical locales, paid medical bills and bought groceries. But there it was, even ten years later. That black cloud of being a car salesman. The sins of the father (those who sold cars before me) are visited upon the sons. It says so in the Bible, Exodus 34:6-7, but it's that damn Hollywood that will never let us forget. Hey, I've got an idea! Let's gang up on Hollywood! Sometimes it works for politicians and it always works for the pious religious right! William Shakespeare did a little play called *Hamlet Prince of Denmark* and wrote "Tis too much proved that with devotion's visage and pious action, we do sugar o're the Devil himself". He was an OK writer too. It was really cool when *V* used the quote in the movie *V for Vendetta* right before he clubbed a bad guy in the head.

I know, I'll start a movement. But all successful movements have catchy names. Some names can even be the opposite of what they really are. For example, "The Clean Air Act" that actually allowed an increase in carbon emissions or the group named Focus on the Family that spends much of their time and resources attacking other families that don't conform to their version of a family. Then there's the "No Child Left Behind Act" that saw drop-out rates increase meaning more children were left behind. I know, I'll call it the "Screw All Car Salesman and Create World Peace Group". Who could be against world peace? Not me, that's for sure.

Next I'll set up a non-profit that pays me a handsome salary to be it's Chairman. Our slogan could be "Peace Through Fair Dealings" and all the car dealers could be donors because they want world peace too. Salespeople could donate money to become honorary members and show their customers that they want world peace. What customer wouldn't want to support world peace, right? They could wear buttons and arm bands to show solidarity. We could march on Washington demanding better treatment for car salespeople in movies and television…because we want world peace. What democratic government wouldn't want to support world peace, right? They could have Congressional hearings and create sub-committees that could have more hearings to create a national holiday for cars salespeople….because they want world peace, right? Why didn't I think of this sooner. Thanks honey!

I wonder if people who sell other things feel the same way? Do all people who ask for money in exchange for products or services share that feeling sometime? I am sure by now that my bias has begun to show, but while our forefathers may have brought this wrath upon us, some salespeople, with the help of their customers, perpetuate the cycle. I remember one customer told me he didn't want to screw around! He wanted my best price and he would buy or leave! So with due diligence I went to my manager and told him exactly what the customer said and he gave me a very aggressive, low number. I believed the customer. When I presented the number to the customer he studied it for a while, leaned back in his chair and said "that looks pretty good. Tell your boss to knock off another five hundred and we've got a deal." Knock off another five hundred dollars? He told me he didn't want to "screw around." When I reminded him of what he told me, he kind of smiled and said "You know how this works. I lie to you, you lie to me." Huh?! I believed him. And what was really ironic was when I told him that I believed him, he didn't believe me. He didn't believe that I believed him. What is that supposed to mean? This went on for a few more minutes and he didn't buy the car.

I could write enough stories like this to fill another book if that guy Shakespeare hasn't already beaten me to it. Maybe it is actually cooler to married to William Shakespeare?

The Saturday Morning Meeting

What's better than a room full of salesmen? A room full of car salesmen who came in a half an hour early on a Saturday and are sure they know everything you're going to tell them anyway. Talk about a motivated group of people! I remember reading in one of my books on sales management that it's impossible to motivate someone. The best a manager can do is create an environment where they can find motivation within themselves. The bottom line is that external motivation lasts only as long as the motivating force is present. Real motivation comes from within you. Wow, thanks for that golden nugget! Now what do I do with a room full of car salesman who are here a half an hour early on a Saturday and are sure they know everything I'm going to tell them?

That did, however, help me understand why some old-school managers motivate their staff by sticking a boot up their ass and yelling all the time. The motivation only lasts as long as the external motivating force is present (i.e. sticking a boot up your ass). But that's not my style. I have always hated those kinds of managers and I didn't want to morph into one of them. My question still remained unanswered.

I remember when I walked into my first meeting as a sales manager for a dealership. The same faded posters on minimum wage, equal opportunity and job safety were pinned to the bulletin board that nobody read. I remember the looks on their faces. There were salesmen who resented the fact that I got promoted and those that thought they were made men because we had worked well together as salesmen before. Staring at the same table and chairs that I sat in just a week earlier, everything I had planned to say, all the pearls of wisdom I wished to depart evaporated like water in the Mojave Desert at high noon. Thirty minutes had passed in an instant and as eternity and the dry erase board was still blank as were the looks on everyone's faces. I remember saying "um" a lot and by the end of the meeting the salesmen were doodling on their Styrofoam coffee cups. Good job!

I had been a manager for years, but these guys were different. Good salespeople have naturally strong personalities and these guys had thick skins from selling cars. I know. I had felt the same way in the same lunch/conference room just a week before when I was a salesman. Every once in a while the owner would attend to tell us how much we were appreciated closely followed with the fact that if we don't like it here, we can leave. Or worse, the owners kid would show up and tell us fake stories about how hard he worked when he was a salesman under the premise that would motivate us to be like him. Somehow I don't think we would get deals spoon fed to us by our fathers, back-talk customers if they said things we didn't like and never have to worry about job security while collecting a fat paycheck. No, with those options off the table, I would have to come up with another game plan.

Thinking back to my time on the sales floor, when things got slow we harassed and made fun of each other mercilessly. Not only did it pass the time, it broke the silence and got everyone's attention too. The slightest misstep, mispronounced word or clothing faux pas was fodder for the rest of the day. So I started to inject a little humor in the Saturday meeting. Anyone who started to drift away would be my target. When a salesman came in with jet black hair after his wife convinced him he would look younger, the first words out of my mouth was "Who's the new guy?" That was followed by ten minutes of the best, and worst, Count Dracula impressions from the other salesman. One salesman stole the show with an imitation of the Count from Sesame Street. "One gray hair, Ah, Ah, Ah. Two gray hairs, Ah, Ah.Ah" and so on.

Getting the meetings back under control and actually reinforcing a skill or teaching them something they didn't know is another issue. I mean what we do is not rocket science. It's pretty basic, actually. But so is driving to work everyday and that's what I often compare selling process to. Most new car salesman hit the floor armed with the "basics." Experienced salesman usually started their new job falling back on the basics until they figure out we do things. The problem is that both types fall into shortcuts. Lets suppose that a salesman sold a car without a demonstration drive. That's now become the bar or the norm. The result is many sales in their first month, or what we call "the honeymoon," and declining sales from there unless they can un-learn the bad habit or short-cut. Now how is that like driving to work everyday? You have that one drive into work where you made every light, didn't get stuck behind any knuckleheads and shaved five minutes off your commute. That suddenly becomes the new amount of time it takes to get to work and you leave the house five minutes later from now on. Why? Because you did it before and that's the new norm. Unless this person un-learns this new behavior, they will always be late for work. The same situation occurs when we sell a car despite our many mistakes. Thank God we can sell cars by accident because a lot of salesman don't sell them on purpose.

Over and over the basics we went. "They want to buy a car. We want to sell a car. Let's just get out of our own way!"

Then I asked for a critique from one of the veterans and he didn't hold back. After listing a myriad of things he thought were wrong, he said something that stuck with me. He said he was tired of the same old thing. He wants something new. He was from the church of *What's Happenin' Now.* And that's exactly what he got. What they got. I showed up at the next meeting in a black suit and a black shirt with a white collar I had cut out from paper. I drank a couple Red Bulls and I was ready to go. The normal silence that I was used to filled the room, but today it was silence and shock as I walked in dressed like a priest/minister. I didn't even tell my other sales manager what I had planned if you could call it planning. What started as a tongue-in-cheek ten commandments of sales from the *Church of What's Happenin' Now* quickly digressed into a bad version of Jesse Jackson's voice along with the fake laying-on of hands I had seen on the Earnest Angely show (don't even get me started on that snake oil salesman). Before I knew it I was casting out the demons of poor customer service asking for help from everyone to lay their hands on a salesman who had been known to stretch the truth a little too far. I did everything except pass the collection plate. The only other thing missing was the hidden 60 Minutes camera to take me out of context and boost ratings with a show about culturally insensitive and evil car salesman.

Thirty minutes flew buy and I had a room full of jovial, pumped-up salesmen. Was it divine inspiration, bad taste or just a willingness to make an idiot out of myself. Well, I didn't see any burning bushes and I didn't get any stone tablets so I'll go with the later two choices.

What Not to Say on a Dealership Interview

We have all been on interviews before. You're nervous and you want them to like you, right? Most managers and/or supervisors ask the same old stale questions. "Where do you see yourself five years from now?" or "Why do you think you would be a good (fill in the blank)?" And I think most hiring decisions are made on an emotion, not on solid information. Maybe that's why so many people are unhappy in their jobs. Most are either under-employed or the job is beyond their skill level. Both situations lead to employee frustration and high turn-over rates. As a manager I have always tried to get the prospective employee to talk and open up. When I do that, it's amazing what people will say. In sales, we are constantly thrown curve balls by our customers and you need to be prepared to think well on your feet.

I have been a manager twenty out of the last twenty-four years and I've always said I could write a book about the ridiculous things people say when they are being interviewed. What a coincidence, I am writing a book, but I don't think I could fill all the pages on this subject alone. Again, I digress. Just like the people I interview who say things I'm sure, had they thought it out, might have worded a little differently.

So there I am, in a suit and tie and most of the interview candidates have been waiting nervously. The people who arrive on time are not made to wait. Those who arrive early are met with at the scheduled time and thanked for being early. Those who are late and did not call can wait an eternity and when I do finally sit down with them, the first question I ask them is why are you late and why didn't you call. It's all down hill from there.

In the normal course of an interview a lot of questions and comments are made from both sides of the desk. Borrowing a format I saw in Al Franken's *Lies, and the Lying Liars Who Tell Them*, I would like to try to bring some of items from sales interview's into perspective (thanks Mr. Franken).

*Saying you're motivated—**Good**

*Actually being motivated—**Better**

*Asking about benefits—**Fine**

*Saying you need the job because you're having surgery and need health benefits—**Bad**

*Not having any health coverage—**Worse**

*Misrepresenting your past experience—**Might work, but bad**

*Not researching the plausibility of your false claims—**Stupid**

*Asking about the hours—**Fine**

*Asking how much you'll get paid—**Zero. You haven't been offered the job yet. Remember, you can turn down the offer**

*Saying you LOVE cars—**Bad**

*Saying you always wanted to sell cars—**Probably not true, but good**

*Saying you LOVE selling cars—**Great**

*Saying you want to sell cars to promote world peace—**The best**

After twenty-plus years conducting hundreds of interviews

I've come to the conclusion that it's mostly a guessing game anyway. People who have made a career in human resources are probably cringing if they're reading this, but I am speaking from my own personal experiences. All the great questions worded to uncover hidden traits and personality tests designed to ferret -out the truth just don't amount to much until the person starts. Only then will you really know if you made the right call. And references are usually more unreliable than the interview process.

Personally, what I'm really looking for is a person's ability to sell themselves to me. That's all that interviews really are, right? You try to convince the employer that you are a better risk than the other guy and not saying stupid things.

Meet the Owner's Son
An Exercise in Restraint

It's time for me to introduce you to the Owner's son. Did he have a college degree? Yes. Did he get his Phd? It was his birth rite. You see his *Pop Had a Dealership*. It was his destiny to someday become our fearful leader. When I was on the selling floor he was one of three sales mangers before his ascension to General Manager and Vice President of the dealership his dad had built. When Phd was the only one to work your deal with you tried your best to keep things simple. His short temper and arrogance had killed many a deal. Working deals with him would be avoided at all costs and I'm pretty sure he secretly liked it that way. It meant he would spend less time working and create more free time for organizing the paperclip pocket of his desk tray or whatever was his fixation de jour. Though he stood about 5' 11" tall with a quasi-athletic build, he oozed squirreliness from every pore in his body. He was the true essence of a real paper tiger. He was one of those guys that talked tough because he went to the gym twice a week, but had probably never actually gone fisticuffs his whole life. Unless someone had decided to kick his ass in high school (but that's just speculation). His clothes and shoes were always clean and neat which looked wonderful with the same hair cut since he has had since he was five years old. Every two weeks he had a standing appointment with the same barber at exactly the same time. It was a buzz cut that was the same length all over. Did I mention that his personality was dominantly obsessive-compulsive?

One of the longest running gags in the store capitalized on his OCD. The dealership had won an award that was prominently displayed in the show room. As if it was his mission in life, he could not walk past it without making sure it was perfectly aligned. So of course, every time he wasn't looking, one of the salesmen would shift it ever so slightly askew. This went on for months. We would move it just to see the frustrated look on his face when he fixed it. We would move it. He would fix it. We would move it. He would fix it. Sometimes three or four times a day.

It was his phone call that prompted my family's move back to our home state. They even paid for the move back and that started my journey as their indentured servant.

What followed was one of the most intense and politically charged mazes I have ever run in my professional career. It's a good thing I was still young enough to endure and naive enough not to know better. I came back as a sales manager and the other sales manager, who I would later nickname Bobble-Head, thought he had it made. He thought I would do the lion's share of the work to impress my new bosses. He was half right. I did the lion's share of the work to help the salespeople put food on their tables, or as Gorge W. Bush put it, "…put food on their families". "W" was quite the orator. After The Holy See, Pope John Paul passed away and was replaced with this new guy, Pope Benedict, I realized that my boss, my Pope and my president were idiots.

After a year I decided that I had made them enough money to pay my servant debt and finally get paid what I was worth at another dealership that had been courting me. And as quickly as turning on a light, I was suddenly worth more to them as well. Part of me rues that day because stay or go, money became my new master. The money and the team of salespeople I had worked so hard to cultivate. And worst of all is that Phd and his father knew it. They knew my wife has had health issues and our two youngest children have some special medical needs as well. Maybe I'm giving them too much credit. Maybe I'm being paranoid. Maybe not. Phd may not have been smart enough to have consciously put it together, but I'm sure his business savvy father was.

Now every single day is an exercise in restraint. If you've actually paid attention to what I'm writing you may have picked up on my sarcasm and disdain for my bosses. And I hate feeling this way because I've had the pleasure and honor of working for great managers. Managers who could teach me because they knew more than me and now I knew what I was missing.

To top things off, Phd has parental issues with his dad, he really thinks he earned his position when the truth is that most of us who work for him have forgotten more about the car business and customer relations than he knows now or will ever learn because, if you think you know it all, you have nothing else to learn. I know it sounds harsh, perhaps a little jaded, but his arrogance has cost everyone, including his father money. His father may consider it guilt money. Money for all the missed dinners and late nights. Money for all the sporting events he didn't attend and money for leaving his son's mother. But I spent too much of my time screwing the salespeople's head's back on and running interference to sustain his enormous ego. Still the business grew despite him, not because of him. Every time he starts a sentence with, "When I was a salesman…", recites a fake memory, parrot's his father's words or starts quoting the last article he read in Automotive News, it's all I can do not to throttle him. If not physically, at least chastise him verbally.

When I would arrive home late with my neck tie loosened, my shoulders slumped my very understanding wife would ask about my day knowing the litany of stories to come that she has heard a hundred times before. When I'd confide and complain she would say "Why didn't you say this…" or "Why didn't you tell him like it really is." And she would be right, but I would just tell her that I would…on my last day. I don't know how I'm going to fit it all in on my last day. Maybe I'll make a list. If I don't do that, this book would certainly do the job or undo my job depending on your perspective. Until then, restraint is the key to my professional survival, though it may eventually lead to my head exploding off my shoulders.

Meet the Management

When I decided to switch dealerships I had to get used to a whole new style of ownership and management. Bobble-Head was my sales manager when I was selling and he "trained" Phd *before* Phd became our boss. That would explain a lot right there. After I became a sales manager I gave him the nickname Bobble-Head because the more he got worked up, the more his head would bobble in a circular motion. It wasn't a "yes" motion and it wasn't a "no" motion. It was a bobble-head motion. You see, he had perfected the art of going whatever direction the ownership's mighty winds would blow him. If they were upset he could nod yes in agreement and no in disbelief at the same time. It was perfect because it was always more important to him to be liked than respected. It may have also been cultivated by giving into his much younger trophy wife's every whim. Even when she eventually left him and took everything, and I mean back-the-truck-up and take everything, he gave in to her every wish. Through his divorce, meltdown and the ensuing Xanax-induced comas, he could do no wrong in the eye's of ownership. In fact, he tried to quit and parlayed that disaster into a part-time position with the dealership, great pay, no weekends and no accountability. No wonder I can't stand him. I console myself by supposing that he has pictures of the owners with farm animals. Am I a little bitter? Oh yeah. Not only did I cover his ass during his many personal crises, I later realized he wouldn't hesitate to throw me under the bus if it suited his agenda. What ever that was. I have his old job now and I firmly believe that he would have it back if the sales department hadn't grown so much while he was drooling on himself.

We haven't even visited the office, Parts department or Service department yet. Walk with me, will you? As I write this I am detecting a troubling pattern. Every manager that "works" here, save one in my sales department, keeps their job with lackluster performance and major ass-kissing, back-stabbing and an unwillingness to work with the sales department as a whole. As an example of the office's ambivalence toward the sale department, any time my department needed office supplies I had to ask for them and some malcontent in the office would begrudgingly get them for me. When I had the audacity to ask for staples, they didn't give me a box of staples. No, no, no. They gave one strip of staples! There are seven staplers in my department!

The final straw that broke the proverbial camel's back happened on a Saturday when no one from the office was in. We needed temporary license plates to deliver cars and I couldn't get to them because they were in the supply cabinet and it was under lock and key. So I started calling the office workers at home to find out where the key might have been. After all, customers who spend $30,000 are kind of funny about having a temp tag so they can drive the car they just bought. When I finally reached someone from the office, she told me she didn't know where the key to supply cabinet was because the office manager hides the key in a different spot every night. We're talking about fucking paper clips here people! I proceeded to explain, in a not very nice way, that I had access to millions of dollars in inventory and tens of thousands of dollars every day, but I couldn't get access to a fucking paper clip on a Saturday?! Of course, first thing Monday morning when the office manager heard what had happened and what was said, she went straight over Phd's head to the owner. With both barrels loaded she detailed the events of the past weekend and the outrageous things I said. I wish I could have been a fly on the wall when he told her I was absolutely right and to give both sales managers a key to her coveted supply cabinet.

That was good for almost a year's worth of the silent treatment. I guess it was really a win-win situation for me. I got a key and I didn't have to act my way through small talk with her.

The service and parts managers are just a variety of human parasites that live off of the sales department. The principles of free trade and healthy competition go right out the window with these two guys because we have to buy all our parts to fix our cars from the parts department and we have to pay above average retail for all of our service. This just shifts money from one column (my column) to another (their column), but what Phd fails to realize is that his system eliminates the need for them to find the best deals when their number one customer, the sales department, can't go anywhere else. I paid more than customers! The service manager actually bragged to me that they were having their best year ever when these policies were put in place. It really is a good thing that I don't own a gun.

One time the service department handed me an estimate for $597 for four tires. Labor not included. When I questioned the price, I was told that the sales department only paid 10% over cost. A few salesmen started to migrate over to the sales desk to see what was going on. I grabbed the closest phone book, opened up the yellow pages to the tire section, covered my eye's and let my finger land on a random tire dealer. One or two more sales people show up. I called that tire store on speaker-phone and found the same tires for $342. Now the cost to the parts department, if they were telling me the truth, was $537.30. That's $195.30 over what any person off the street would pay at the tire store I randomly pick with my eyes closed! Now I'm not a rocket scientist, but I'm pretty sure that saving the dealership $195.30 is a good thing. So why aren't they shopping around for the best deal? They don't have any incentive. The sales department has to pay what ever they ask for. When word of my price shopping exercise got back to the ownership, Phd was pissed. I tried to explain that I was trying to save the dealership money. It ended with me getting reprimanded for undermining the parts and service manager's authority in front of the employees. That's pure motivation, again.

My Hawaiian Vacation

For months I waited for this vacation. When it got closer to the departure date I started crossing off the days on the calendar. Then the day finally came. When I arrived, I was greeted by a sea of smiling faces. Everyone seemed so relaxed. It could only be described as a calm electricity or energy. Personally, I was giddy. I arrived at work and I knew that Phd wouldn't be there. You see, I wasn't going to Hawaii, but he was, and that meant I was on vacation from him. For one glorious week I didn't have to act interested in his stupid stories or listen to him whine about everything from getting paged before 10:00 am to how he needs to leave early to clear his head. He told me once that he does his best thinking on his sofa while watching television. I had heard that same line before. It wasn't dejavu. It was the same thing my sixteen-year-old daughter would say to me when she was told to turn off the television and concentrate on her homework. Now I love my daughter more than life itself, but I understand that she's sixteen and I expect that kind of reasoning from her.

Unlike my daughter though, I can't say things to Phd like "Do I have stupid written on my forehead?" or "I was born at night, but it wasn't last night" or "You're grounded!" But now that I think about it, he acts much worse that any teenager that my wife and I have ever reared and we've done it four times. With that in mind, I've created the Top Ten Reasons to Ground Your Boss;

10.) Pouting and slamming doors.

9.) Not doing their homework and not completing assignments.

8.) Tardiness.

7.) Cutting out early.

6.) Lying.

5.) Making rules and setting policies they won't adhere to.

4.) Dress code violations.

3.) Acting like he came up with your ideas.

2.) Not leading by example.

1.) WHINING!

I mean real whining. Whining that would put any teenage girl to shame.

Whining about how hard he works to his personal life or how he can't listen to *Sade* at work because that's the music he plays at home when he's trying to convince his wife to give in to pathetic pleas for sex. The whole time I'm forced to act as though I actually sympathize with his situation. He has even gone as far as to complain about how much he hates the car business. In a rare, unguarded moment, he once told me he wished he could just take the share of the business he's earned and get out of the dealership. I still haven't figured out how he'll live on $3.47. Of course you and I both know that number, right or wrong, will have a lot more zeros attached to it. Then I would have the privilege to interview for my own job with the new owners. I guess I should be careful what I wish for, but with the huge advance I'll get for writing this book and the commission from all sales, it won't matter. Right?

For now I'll just enjoy my vacation. Eight days without Phd. My Hawaiian vacation, without the sun and sand or the stress he brings to my everyday.

Uniforms: A Nun in Purgatory

I spent my elementary school days in a Catholic school. Dark blue pants with the knees worn from hours on the asphalt playground and the light blue button-down oxford shirt. To complete the ensemble, and just to make sure that we stood out enough from our public school counterparts, the third generation clip-on tie that had been chewed on in many a boring math class by my two older brothers before me. Back then most of the teachers were nuns. Real nuns, not the "everybody-knows-I'm-a-nun-anyway-street-clothes-wearing" type nuns that taught my daughter for eight years. I will spend the balance of this book sharing re-run Catholic school stories. No, I'm just kidding. Okay, maybe just one.

The classroom was like any other in 1969 Main Street America. The waxed asbestos laden tile floor that met the tanish colored glazed block, which went six rows high on the wall. From there the walls were painted a very pale yellow, or maybe it was a very pale green. It's hard to recall, for all I know it was a very pale blue. Those were the only colors used back then and they were covered with blackboards, bulletin boards and posters relating to our subjects or the mission work to save the "pagan babies" in third world countries. You see, the way it was explained to us third graders was that God was calling us to give our pocket change to the missionaries who would baptize the "pagan babies" and then they could get into heaven. That sounds pretty cut and dry, but when one of the kids asked what happened to the "pagan babies" who died before they could be baptized, Sister Katherine looked down. All I could see was the top of her black habit (a habit is a nun hat for all the non-Catholic and "pagan babies" who might read this book). Her pause was thoughtful and seemed deeply contemplative and lasted for what felt like hours as we all waited on the edge of our wooden desk seats to discover the fate of these pitiful beings. Then, clutching the crucifix on the rosary she wore around her neck, she looked us in the eye and explained that their souls would spend eternity wandering aimlessly looking for redemption in Purgatory and never see the face of God. She then consoled our stunned faces with the fact that because they were too young to commit sin they would not go to hell and burn for all eternity. You can imagine my sense of relief. I did not realize at the time that I would grow up and work 58 hours a week in Purgatory. Of course given the alternative, I suppose I could have done worse.

Despite all you hear, the education I received was excellent with uniforms and all. But when Phd decided that the sales team should wear uniform shirts so that the staff would always look professional, all those memories came flooding back. Not the ones about "pagan babies" and crucifixes. The memories about the countless hours we all spent trying to think up new ways to bend the uniform dress code without getting in trouble with Sister Katherine. I remembered how the boys who wore ties, that they would knot themselves, would make the ties really short so that the tie would only reach halfway down their shirt. When a new policy banned ties that were too short they responded by making them extra long. I understood this pattern of behavior and I knew my guys would do exactly the same thing.

As I watched his lips move while he adjusted his glasses non-stop I didn't hear a word past "uniforms". "Blah, blah, blah…uniforms…blah, blah, blah…dress code…blah, blah, blah". In my mind all I could see was the initial revolt against whatever he decided they should wear, then the capitulation before they would eventually start to bend the rules. As it was with most company policies, someone else would suggest it and I would have to enforce it. "Think fast", I told myself as Phd blew the non-existent dust off his lenses and adjusted them again. What would satisfy his desire for the uniformed look and be virtually unbendable as a dress code. His lips kept moving and I knew he already had something in mind. But before I could think of something, he said "blah, blah, blah…I'm thinking bright red shirt".

Bobble-head sat next to me bobbing his head as I visualized a showroom awash with over-laundered pink shirts. Oh yeah, that looks great. "What about light blue?" I thought. No, that wouldn't do because the manufacture's colors were red, black and white. If red became pink, then black would become gray. That leaves white. Now, as his lips moved, I could see portly salesmen in wrinkled white shirts instead of wrinkled pink shirts. It's not perfect, but it is better, and now I would have to lead Phd to the conclusion that white was a better choice so it could be his idea or at least his decision.

Crisp white shirts with a logo became the new uniform. Pants must be pressed and worn with dress shoes. Let the games begin! Months down the road as I cajoled and threatened and coerced dress code compliance it occurred to me that I had become Sister Katherine! A nun! A nun wandering aimlessly in purgatory searching for redemption.

Happy

Happy. That's what the salespeople called me. Of course it was with their not-so affectionate sarcasm. I used to be happy at work. Really, I was happy most of the time. Maybe not skipping-through-fields-of-flowers happy, but I had a lot to be happy and content about. I had a great marriage to my beautiful wife, our four wonderful kids and enough money to cover most of the bills. It was as close to the American dream as most people get. That was before I became a sales manager at the auto dealership.

I have always aspired to become more than whatever position I was hired in to do. When I was going to college I was working full-time as a clerk at the local convenience store. It was called The Open Pantry. I wanted to own one. I went as far as inquiring about purchase the store I worked in because the store was owned by the parent company at the time. It's a good thing that God doesn't answer all your prayers. If He had, I'd be selling thick sliced bologna by the pound instead of collecting fat royalty checks for this book.

The next job I was hired to do was checking stock at Saks Fifth Avenue. It worked out great with my full-time college load because they didn't care when I worked as long as I got in forty hours of stocking in goods. You would be amazed at how much rich people pay for bobbles, clothes and useless trinkets. Now, it's important to remember to pronounce the name Saks Fifth Avenue through clenched teeth with your nose slightly elevated. Or if you really want to do it right, you simply call it "Saks". I went there faithfully, day after day, tagging clothes that cost more than I would make in a month. On the bright side, I did get a 20% employee discount that I could not afford to use. From the dock I moved to the cosmetics stockroom where I got my first exposure to commission sales. Over forty commissioned salespeople comprised of 39 women and to men who might have wished they were women. Not only did they get paid by the hour, but also they would get one to three percent of their sales! Wow, one to three percent! Within a month I knew everyone's life story and I never had to ask a single question. I would just work quietly in the stockroom pricing cologne and lipsticks and listening to the salespeople talk.

But my greatest leap toward happiness requires me to fast-forward four years. I was now the assistant manager/buyer in cosmetics and I was assigned the grueling task of scheduling the store's models to spray customers with cologne and pass out samples. Not the kind you see, and avoid, today. Real fashion models, who otherwise wouldn't give me the time of day if I met them on the street. That's right, the stock boy was now working with real fashion models and I thought I was the man. But like every job, what seemed great at first quickly became mundane, then tedious, and then a complete pain in the ass. That was until the day that changed my life forever.

Christian Dior was launching their new fragrance called *Poison* in Saks stores across the country. The Fashion Office had hired a new petite model and asked me to schedule her in the rotation. Christian Dior's sales representative had dropped off a box of peacock feathers and the outfit they wanted their models to wear. It was this ridiculous looking turban with a peacock feather and a fake, I'm sorry, faux ruby on the forehead. The model was to spray the perfume on the iridescent blue and green peacock feathers from the box and give them to customers. Sounds perfect for the new kid. I gave the outfit to the Fashion Office and asked them to send her down at noon. Twelve o'clock arrived and down the escalator came a 5'5" vision of beauty that made that ridiculous turban look mysterious and captivating. At least I was captivated. I couldn't take my eyes off her, until she looked over and I quickly looked away like a twelve-year-old schoolboy. I found myself looking for excuses to walk past her or work on a display near her. Yeah, I was the man alright.

Now I'm sitting here twenty years later, our youngest daughter is a junior in high school and that mysterious turban-wearing vision of beauty has been my wife for close to twenty years. Instead of forty commissioned cosmetic saleswomen I'm managing fourteen car salespeople and I'm not sure which I prefer. Well that's not exactly true. The money is much better but the hours still suck and customers never change (more on that topic later).

It was a car salesman who first called me "Happy". I'll admit that I can be sullen and sober, sarcastic and smart-assed, but I have my moments of cheer as well. But he never let up. It was always "hey Haps, lets work a deal'' or "hey Hapster, check out this trade-in" or "Haaaapy" if he really wanted to get under my skin. You see, he had found the perfect nickname for a boss. It wasn't a slur or profane. The word happy by itself wasn't derogatory and it sounded juvenile to tell someone "stop calling me happy!" Soon most of the salesman started calling me Happy as well and not much later I started answering to my new moniker. In hindsight, I have been called worse things those who have worked for me.

Take Your Daughter to Work Day

My daughter is more like me than I would care to admit. At times she's too much like me for her own good. Sometimes she's too much like her mother for her own good, but most of the time she's a better person than I. When she was in sixth grade she came home with a permission slip to be excused from all her classes on Take-Your-Daughter-to-Work-Day. I was wrestling with the idea of exposing her to the showroom for a whole day. My guys are usually very well behaved around each other's kids, but could I reasonably expect them to last an entire day.

Suddenly a lot of other questions began to swirl around in my head. Does she have any notions about what daddy does for a living? I know she has seen how car guys are portrayed on television. You know what I'm talking about. Slick hair, plaid suit, white shoes with a matching belt and sunglasses.

"What's it gonna' take to put you in this cream puff of a car today?"

"This baby was driven by a little old lady to church on Sundays."

"Yeah, I know it's got 100,000 miles. Her church was far away."

I can tell you honestly that in all the years that I've been in the car business, I've never heard anyone say that to a customer. That being said there is plenty said around the sales desk that I would not want my daughter to hear or behaviors I wouldn't want her to see.

Reluctantly I agreed to let her come to work for the day. I could give her a tour of the building, introduce her to everyone and show her off. Maybe she would really be interested in what I do for a living. I could show her how I inspect and appraise cars. Yeah, that's right. I could show her how important math skills are and how you really do use this stuff when you get out of school. Now I was getting excited. I could dispel all those television images that she's been bombarded with. Then I recalled the time her school sent home a note asking parents to come in on Career Day and talk about what they do for a living. I never got called to come and talk. Her teacher must watch too much TV.

The fact of the matter is that those television scenarios came from somewhere. The scenarios don't contain wizards or dragons so they can't all be the work of someone's active and malicious imagination. Something happened to someone at sometime so we're all the same and we all pay the price. A sort of class-action hate suit (and the suit is probably plaid with a white belt and matching shoes). But I do understand. Most of the good salespeople do and try to make the experience enjoyable after doing our penance for someone else's mistakes. Think about it for a minute. You are going to spend, and probably borrow, a lot of money. Upwards to $40,000 or more depending on your selection. Shouldn't you be enjoying it? I know I'm ticked-off if I spend $5.00 dollars for fast food and the fries aren't hot. Maybe a change in perspective is in order. I am not suggesting that anyone "roll-over" and pay whatever for a bad car or bad service, but if you like the vehicle and the salesperson has tried to be helpful, enjoy it for God's sake! There are plenty of ways to make sure you are not paying too much and I'll get to those later. But again, I digress.

After days of fretting and worry, my daughter comes to work with me. She actually seemed excited. Okay, this is going to be good. The first thing she asks me upon our arrival at work at 8:55 a.m. is for money for the snack machine. By 9:30 a.m. she has my password and is playing on the internet and I.M.'ing her friends. Probably about how cool it is to get out of a day of school. At 10:30 a.m. I get the first "I'm bored" so I try to show her what Dad does for a living. 10:35 a.m., "I'm bored." We appraise a car and drive around the block in a filthy '99 Dodge something that smelled like cat pee. Honestly people, clean your cars and have you ever heard of a little known invention called an air freshener? 10:40 a.m., "That's gross and I'm bored." 11:00, "What's for lunch?" I sent someone for Taco Bell after agreeing to pay for their lunch as well. We ate in our small lunch/conference room and she was peppered by questions from my salespeople about me and we had a few laughs. Then at 11:45 I get a droopy, I'm-bored-out-of-my-mind hug and she asks, "Daddy, can Mommy pick me up?" My daughter always adds the "y" at the end of Mom or Dad when she wants sympathy. 12:30 p.m. and she is on her way home with Mom and it occurs to me that after all that worry and contemplation, I was an accomplice to skipping school, but I'm smiling. She's a great kid and she gets great grades and had my job been remotely similar or as interesting as the television version, who knows? Maybe she would have wanted to stay. I don't think she'll be asking anyone "What's it gonna' take to put you in this creampuff of car?" and I'm relieved.

It Could be a Sitcom
(But People Won't Identify with a Car Salesman)

I need a show hands. Who out there enjoyed the movie *Used Cars*? Okay. That's what I expected. Those of you who did see it either thought "OH! That's terrible!" or you said to yourself "I knew it! They're all liars and charlatans!" It epitomizes everyone's conception of the car business. It stars Kurt Russell as a slick car salesman named Rudy Russo who only thinks about himself and his run for the Arizona State Senate. Rudy has the obligatory plaid sport coat and sunglasses and he's going to buy the election, of course. That is until he is side tracked by an even slicker, more evil car dealer, named Roy L. Fuchs (sound it out folks). As the protagonist of the plot, Rudy ends up *kinda* doing the right thing. It's not a family movie to be sure. When a new salesperson has been on the selling floor for a little while they will eventually ask me why people treat them so poorly when all they want to do is help. My response; watch *Used Cars*. I'll even let them borrow my copy. It's got it all, from the plaid sport coats and sunglasses to all the tricks people are sure that we use. Actually, the movie is one of my guilty pleasures because if my conscience won't allow me to commit the sins, at least I can enjoy watching a fictional version of someone else doing it. But we do have enough odd characters as customers walking through our doors and the sit-com could feature them.

We have "Wacky Chinese Lady" (my personal favorite), "Coffee Guy" and "Crooked Neck" (not a jab at someone with physical disability because he doesn't have one. He just always tilts his head when you talk to him) just to name a few.

Wacky Chinese Lady just caught my attention when she approached the sales desk demanding service with a voice that carried over all the noise of a bustling showroom. Music, salespeople and customers hummed and then the din was cut by a loud voice with a heavy accent. She told me that her salesman was "sick in the head". Like a glass that falls to the ground at a restaurant and everyone stops what they are doing to see who's to blame. I thought I better get involved because I had a customer problem. Before I could get a word out and before the noise had picked back up, her salesman appeared and asked her if she had been dipping into the ginseng a little too much. Now everyone was watching and listening and no one new what was going on. She might have been five feet tall, but she commanded attention with her presence, personality, volume and bag lady clothing accented with one inch long gray roots which met the balance of her artificially jet-black hair. In what seemed like an eternity, I struggled to understand what she was saying while not being distracted by her infectious, half-crazed laugh and she was swinging a brochure at the salesman and me like an old-world grandmother who wants the kids to behave. It was hard not to join in the laughter. She was yelling in very broken English. She was swinging wildly and I didn't know how to resolve the situation.

I didn't even understand the situation. All I could do was keep my arms up and try to talk to her. Finally, when her arms got tired, I was able to decipher that all she wanted to do was buy a car that was not a "bad luck" color. Not your usual request, but very important to her. In another chapter I lament how some customers reserve their bad behavior just for us in the car sales. She was the exception. On a family trip to the local indoor shopping mall I saw her passing out samples in the mall's food court harassing passers-by who didn't want to try the chicken and chasing away the kids who had already tried one. For the next four years she would make her monthly pilgrimage to my office to ask what the unpaid balance of her loan was. Over that time she got to meet my wife and family on several occasions, and always came out swinging. Maybe she did dip into the ginseng a little too much. I miss her.

Then there was coffee guy. He would come in several times a week, always in the morning, wearing an old jacket from the Army-Navy store, grab five or six brochures and head for the coffee in the customer waiting area. The coffee was free. It became a rite of passage for all new salespeople to ask if he needed help. The veterans knew better. Any conversation would quickly turn to his ten year old truck that, the way he described it, would never die. As if it had been forged by the gods on Mount Olympus themselves. Having experienced it first hand when I was a salesman I knew the conversations never lasted less than fifteen minutes or longer than an eternity.

Documenting his pattern of behavior, one salesperson started to take his mooching personally. Almost as though he was paying for the coffee out of his paycheck. So upon seeing his truck pull in, he would run and hide the Styrofoam coffee cups. We would watch him grab four or five brochures, there were too many of those to hide, and he would make his way to the waiting area and stand there. Dumbfounded, he would look at the other customers enjoying their coffee in our cups and search the vicinity for more. Childish and immature? Yes. Satisfying? Absolutely. He had him. After years of free coffee and enough brochures to wallpaper the lower level of his house, he had him. But like most of God's creatures, he evolved and adapted. The only thing funnier than watching Coffee Guy look for more cups was the look on my salesman's face when he started to bring in his own mug. And just a closing note; the coffee is not that good.

The last customer I've chosen to share with you is Crooked Neck and let me reiterate that he does not have a physical or mental handicap that forces his head to one side. We call him Crooked Neck because he hasn't given anyone his name and over the years has taken hours of time from the sales staff with his questions about the cars. When he would ask a question he had a habit of completely tilting his head to one side as those he was discussing the most serious issues of the day. He would ask about cruise control with the earnest inflection of someone trying to solve the Middle East crisis or world hunger. At the point of writing this I have been at the dealership for over ten years and he has never bought anything. Maybe he's lonely or maybe he really is that interested in cruise control. We'll never know. We'll just keep letting the new guys answer all his questions. I just tell myself that he'll have to buy a car sooner or later.

Does any of this sound like sit-com material to you? Now don't go acting all holier-than-thou. I'm sure everyone who is reading this book has a similar experience at work that they can relate to. Maybe you have the stuff of the next "Seinfeld", you just haven't written it down yet.

The Truth About Salespeople Who Lie

You can dress salespeople in a uniform so they all look the same, but getting everyone to behave in a consistent, informed and honorable manner is something quite different. Salespeople, a group in which I am proud to include myself, are a largely likeable lot. Good salespeople can converse with just about anyone under just about any circumstances; a skill not found in the public at large. If you take most folks out of their group of like-minded people and out of their comfort zone, they clam up faster than a felon without an alibi. A salesperson that has not mastered the art of conversation is almost too painful to watch. I said almost because it can be a spectator sport if you know what to watch for. Ask anyone in an electronics store for help and pursue a conversation and you'll see what I mean. As a rule, I'm a lay-down for most salespeople if they provide a modicum of service or information. Hell, I don't even hang-up on telemarketers. But when I'm shopping, occasionally I'll toy with one like a cat does with a mouse it has cornered, keeping them out of their comfort zone until that small bead of perspiration forms along their hairline or upper lip area.

That's when it happens. That's the point where even Mother Theresa would begin telling "untruths". I've carefully chosen the word "untruth" over the term lie for a reason. When it comes to sales the difference is as large as the Grand Canyon. The fact is that most people who are on the spot and out of their comfort zone will say the next thing that pops into their head. It's not that they want to lie, they just don't know the answer and they make one up to avoid looking stupid. Most salespeople don't start out as liars, the lazy ones just sort of morph into them. Then again, I have worked with guys who seemed incapable of telling the truth.

One such salesman was Donk. Not only was he a habitual liar, his personal hygiene was a real treat. Donk was in his late 40's when I first met him, although he looked much older. His thinning hair was greasy and flaky with the appearance that he had combed it over with a piece of buttered toast. The hair he had was the light brown color of Grecian Formula where it met the off-white bushy hair on the back of his unshaved neck. Every white piece of clothing he owned was dingy and permanently wrinkled. Maybe he made his whites dingy to hide all the pet hair from home. He was a sight with his potbelly and his dingy white athletic socks that he wore inside out because he had already worn them once right side out. To this day it amazes me that he sold anything, but he did. And his customers loved him.

I don't know if his inability to tell the truth stemmed from a deep-seated need to be liked and accepted or if it was just pathological. Either way, I don't believe he could help himself. I do remember the day I was sure that he had told the truth. He had been working with the other manager, Bobblehead, to resolve a customer problem of his own making. I was sort of half listening because to try to comprehend and sort through all the details and lies would give you a headache. Donk was burning his greasy candle at both ends telling the customer anything they wanted to hear and telling Bobblehead something different. Donk was back in the service department lying to his customer when Bobblehead had started to put it all together. He paged him loudly to the office! His head was really bobbing now as he became more impatient waiting for Donk. Feeling he had waited long enough, he flew out of his office to hunt Donk down. Just then Donk came around the corner panicked and stuttering. One by one he was confronted with his lies and half-truths as he made excuses and offered explanations. "I didn't promise the customer a free oil change!" he pleaded and quickly added "the customer just thinks I gave him a free oil change!"

"If you didn't offer a free oil change, why does the customer think you did?!"

More stories flew around until anyone in earshot was thoroughly confused. But no one was more confused than Donk. He had spun so many webs that when Bobblehead, furious and really bobbing now, demanded to know, "Donk, are you lying to me?", he had only one choice left.

"Ah…ah…ah…I don't know!" Donk's last resort was to tell the truth. He really didn't know what was a lie and what was the truth. Donk was living proof that if you repeated a lie often enough it became a personal truth. His subconscious mantra was "It's not a lie if you believe it." You could tell it was painful for him. The truth to Donk was like cryptonite to Superman. It somehow diminished him and made him feel less in control, if that was even possible. I watched these events unfold with the same perverse fascination that makes you try to see something as you pass a car accident. I couldn't look away.

If you are wondering what ever became of Donk, a wealthy relative died and left him over half of a million dollars. This confirms that there is no justice in the world or God has a really bad sense of humor. Donk continued to sell cars after he got his inheritance. I guess there weren't enough people to lie to at home.

What's with the Name Calling?
How to Have a Good Experience Buying a Vehicle

You know what I'm talking about. Don't think I didn't hear you.

"Look at those salesman. They're swarming just like sharks!" Or maybe you said vultures or snakes or wolves. It doesn't matter. We get the message. As salespeople, sometimes we are forced to wait for customers to come. Whether it's a walk-in or "up", or we're waiting for our appointment to show. The customer who claims that they were "jumped on" before they could get out of their car is probably the same person who walks in the showroom asking "What does it take to get some help around here?!" because they have been allowed to look around for five minutes before being approached. Or maybe you're the guy who walks into the showroom and asks, "Who wants sell a car today?" You get the gist.

I've often wondered how these customers behave in other purchasing situations. Do they tell the girl at the grocery check-out to tell her boss that they wont go a penny over .59 cents for the loaf of bread marked $1.79? Or that they want to see the invoice for the gallon of milk before they make an offer. No, they reserve this behavior just for us, the great Satan of the sales profession.

The fact I've come to accept is that salespeople, especially car salespeople, are pretty low on the most-liked list. Right above attorneys. Not that I have anything against attorneys. There are good ones and bad ones just as in any profession.

Here's one for you; What do you call three car salesmen at the bottom of a lake? The answer is; a good start. Ha ha. Here's another one; If a car salesman and an attorney jumped off the roof of a fifty-story building, who would hit the ground first? The answer is; who cares? Get it, who cares?! Pretty funny stuff, right? I've heard them all.

I do not want to pretend that I don't understand where the customer's point of view is coming from. I do, really. Not long ago, I was in line at the grocery store waiting to check out. I had been shopping with my wife and the cart was over-flowing with all the household staples. This is the point where I usually start embarrassing my wife by reading the tabloid headlines out loud to her as if I believed every word. "Honey, the Bat-Boy has children!" or "A potato chip in the shape of the Shroud of Turin has foretold when the world will end! I sure hope no one eats it before all it's mysteries are unlocked!" I would usually keep this up until she would throw some groceries at me or start apologizing to the cashier and the other waiting customers because I'm only allowed out on supervised day-trips.

Today was different. There was a new collection of paperback books that looked to be of the highest quality selling for only $1.99. They were marked down from the whopping cover price of $2.69 or $3.09 if you lived in Canada. Man, those Canadians are always taking it in the shorts. The books covered topics that offered the answers to life's most persistent questions. Questions like how to lose weight while eating ice cream, how to use your horoscope to get rich and the one that caught my eye had the lengthy title of *How to Buy or Lease a Car (or Truck) Without Getting Ripped Off!* That one was published by the prestigious *American Media Mini Mags,* Incorporated. AMI, Inc. has been owned by the *National Enquirer* and *The Globe,* so it is only reasonable to assume that this publication would be chock-full accurate and up-to-date information.

I did what any rational person who reads tabloid headlines aloud would do. I told the cashier to tell her boss that I won't go a penny over $1.50! Not really. I just paid the $1.99 asking price like everyone else. The paperback's cover was festooned with clip-art that included an old car with a broken windshield and a wrecked front end juxtaposed with a balding car salesman in the obligatory plaid sport coat and, of course, white shoes. All harbingers of the information that would spelled-out on the pages within.

Let me start by saying that I have not worked at every car dealership in the country, but I have actually worked in a few dealerships and write from personal experience, not stories and wild windjammers I've heard from others. I'm not so sure the same can be said about the person who penned this piece of trash. After I read the book, I was afraid to go to work! I can only imagine how a potential customer would feel after reading that dealerships fabricate invoices, secretly pipe your private conversations into a manager's office, display pictures of fictional family members or, and I saved my favorite for last, hire a fake customer to strike up a conversation with you to act as though he's angry because he paid more than you for the same car. The only thing this guy left out was the JFK grassy knoll and United States lunar landing that was really filmed in a Hollywood studio. Survey says…total bullshit.

Now for the FACTS about buying a vehicle, minus the conspiracy theories. Here are a few things you need to know AND accept before you hit the car lots.

Don't depend on your salesperson for all the information. Some may have it and some may not. Do some research of your own.

Trust is earned and is a give-and-take process. Find a salesperson that understands this and remember it's a two-way street.

You don't have to tolerate incompetence. Some guides advocate trying to out-smart the salesperson, but in truth a competent salesperson will be there later when you need help and to help you through the sales process now.

Good salespeople don't need to lie and don't let pride get in the way of making a deal. The same can be said of good customers.

If you are researching your car's value on web sites remember that they are averages. If you plug your information into KellyBlueBook.com, NADA.com and Edmunds.com you will get three very different numbers on the SAME car. And last, but certainly not least, when rating your vehicle don't use "excellent" to describe the condition. If it was excellent, you wouldn't be trading it in or you would be selling it to a friend or family member.

KellyBlueBook.com, NADA.com and Edmunds.com will NOT buy your car for the amount they post. In our frustration, salespeople have joked that the customer forgot to hit the "print-my-check" button. They also cannot sell you a car at the prices they post. That will always require a third party, either private or retail.

Ask for a CarFax report on used vehicles before you buy one. A dealer should provide one for free. It's important to know that a vehicle can still have been in an accident or have paint work without the information showing up on a report. Check used vehicles carefully and take long test drives.

Paint work doesn't mean it's a bad car. It just means that the previous owner had some body work done. Be thorough with your inspection.

A dealer must make money on the sale just like your grocer or favorite clothing store must sell their goods at a profit. That being said, you don't want anyone to be able to retire on money made off of you.

AUTOMOBILES ARE A DEPRECIATING ASSETT. Some depreciate faster than others, but they all depreciate. Try to enjoy them and get your use out of them because you are paying for it.

Wow! Wasn't that fun? No? Maybe kinda' sort-of? Maybe not, but it will reduce your frustration and fears if you have them, about buying your next vehicle. And about all this name-calling, remember; Sticks and stones can break my bones....so, please don't throw sticks and stones.

Mochie Christmas

The owner has a life most men would envy, but not me. Am I justifying my station at this time in my life? Maybe, but I don't think so. As the saying goes, "Life abhors a vacuum," and that applies to the space between your ears and the things that you worry about as well. Like me, most people worry about things like my family's health, making the mortgage and getting the cable turned back on before the finale of *Dancing with the Stars*. Just in case this gets published after *Dancing with the Stars* leaves the airwaves, I will enlighten you. *Dancing with the Stars* is a summer fill-in fluke that features B and C-list celebrities paired up with professional dancers who try to teach them how to dance. They compete throughout the season to determine who has improved the most or, just like in high school, who is the most popular. The show is complete with a panel of judges no one has ever heard of until the show premiered. These shows are the perfect distraction from people's every day worries. Now, on the other hand, if you're a dealership receptionist who gets promoted to owner's wife #3, you can imagine all the space in that head for new worries. You can worry about Mochie.

Mochie is "short" for Mocha. She actually said that. Try it once. See how those two syllables roll off the tongue much faster than the other two syllables. My wife and I heard all about it at the manager's Christmas party at the country club where the owner is a member. It's always a very nice affair and a good reason to get dressed-up. Unless' it's a Mochie Christmas. That's the way I'll always remember the Christmas of 2005.

It was colder than normal for a mid-December evening and my wife looked beautiful. She was wearing a black velvet Sgt. Pepper style jacket that she bought specifically for the party. She made the car smell like *Giorgio* and for a few seconds I was 27 again. As we drove up the private lane to the country club we were talking about how this years party might not be as fun as in the past. One of my wife's best friends is married to a man who used to be one of our sales managers. He had left earlier in the year to open a pizza shop and they would not be there tonight to sit with us. In the past, we could always depend on each other if any of us got tired of talking shop. We were each other's wing-men if one of us got trapped in an unbearable conversation.

The valet opened my wife's door when I pulled up to the entrance and I tried to remember if I'm supposed to tip him now to take good car of the car or when we leave after I could see the car was well cared for. I knew I wasn't going to tip both times. My indecision forced me tip when I leave. Listening to myself as I write this I wonder how could something designed to make my life easier can cause me such grief. We checked our coats and made our way down the long, wide hallway to the party. Just like every year before, those who had arrived before us congregated right inside the door instead of moving further into the room, giving me that instant twinge of claustrophobia. I'm not afraid of small places, but I don't like people in my "bubble". The room was large and grand with a big hearth and fireplace that was roaring. The dim lighting made the room very inviting and I never understood why people wouldn't move further into such a nice setting. We shook a couple hands and flagged down the waiter for drinks ASAP. A cosmopolitan graced my wife's hand and I sipped my double rum and coke.

I was halfway through my second drink when the owner and his wife came by during their obligatory rounds through the hired help just as they had done every year before, but this year would be different. As we dispensed with small talk the conversation turned to pet dogs. The owner's wife's eyes lit up as if she had just been told her husband's net worth for the first time. It seems that she had one of those small, expensive hybrids for a pet. It's name was Mocha, or Mochie for short! I must refer to her dog as "it" because I had already started tuning out of the conversation before I learned it's sexual persuasion. She got my attention back when she told my wife that we *have* to sit by her so we could finish the conversation which, roughly translated, means she is going to spend the next hour or so telling us all about Mochie.

Imagine how interesting it was to learn about Mochie's bowel movements. I was just riveted when she explained how she always knew Mochie's poop from the other poop in her yard and about their plans to catch this phantom pooper. Sympathy swelled inside me as she described how worried she was because they had switched dog food and Mochie just didn't seem to be eating as much. Do you know how she knew that? It wasn't by how much food was left in the dish. She could tell by it's poop! I'm the one making a big deal out of this when it was my poor wife who sat right next to her on the Mochie front line the whole time. She was seated on my wife's left and I was on my wife's right. It's funny now, but I felt helpless when she would briefly turn her body toward me with eyebrows raised and a look on her face that either said somebody save me or somebody shoot me. "Mochie wears a sweater". "Mochie rides in my purse." "Mochie is lost without me." "Mochie cured cancer." I made-up that last one.

I think we were both equally taken aback by her declaration that taking care of Mochie carried much more responsibility than raising her daughters. When she noticed the looks on our faces, somewhere between blank and she can't be serious, she rationalized her position. The way she explained it was that if she had drank too much the night before, her daughters could always get their own bowls of dry cereal and watch television, however Mochie required so much more attention. She would actually have to get out of bed, no matter hung-over she was, to let Mochie out to poop. And Mochie couldn't get it's own food or water by itself and she would have to do that too. Mochie couldn't bathe itself either. Let's just say she won't be getting nominated for a "Mother of the Year" award anytime soon.

Another year was coming to a close and this was one more Christmas party for the record books. We were saying our good-byes and I was shaking hands with the owner. Sarcastically I said, knowing he'd be too drunk to remember, "that sounds like one heck of a dog you have there." He smirked and said out of the side of his mouth, "I want to die and be reincarnated as a fucking dog!" The owner has a life most men would envy, but not me.

CPSIA information can be obtained at www.ICGtesting.com
Printed in the USA
LVOW041923110512

281392LV00003B/118/P